The Wisdom of Bees

Up close and personal bee photography,

life lessons, interesting facts, and

questions to ponder...

by Andrea King

Welcome!

I've been taking pictures of bees and flowers for many years now, enjoying the beautiful dance and relationship between them. Recently we discovered a hive of aggressive bees in our back yard. The process of finding someone to humanely relocate them was rewarding and educational. The hive was growing rapidly in a stack of tires I had covered with a tarp. In the process of removal, we were able to take many photos of the combs and bees, even getting a look at the developing larvae, and the emerging adult bee! This book has been created to share some of the wisdom that nature offers us when we take time to observe, and also to give you an intimate look at bees and their work. The experience got us thinking about keeping bees in the future! Until then, I'm excited to present this up close, and personal look at bees doing what they do best.

I'd like to express my gratitude to Dan Punch, www.azhoneybz.com, who gently relocated the bees to a farm where they can be managed and do their work, and also to Mychael Lee, who suited up and took all of the honeycomb and hive photos.

Please enjoy the bees and flowers and the wisdom they share.

Blessings!

Andrea

Dedicated, with love, to Mychael Lee.
Thank you for joining me on this life journey,
contributing your photos, and especially your
support to bring this first book into existence.
I look forward to creating many amazing
publications with you!

Recognize the sweetness found within your heart. You are a teacher and a student, a giver and a receiver in every situation you encounter.

The gift of honey... Sweet nectar goes through quite a remarkable process. It is collected by one worker bee, then transferred to another worker bee in the hive, who "chews" it to partially digest and change the nectar's makeup with enzymes. After it has been processed to a thicker liquid, it is deposited into the honey combs, and fanned by bee wings to encourage evaporation of the water from the honey. Then it is sealed with wax and stored until is is eaten.

Are you taking time to enjoy the sweetness in life?

Pay attention to those who try new things. It takes strength to explore new places and step away from the crowd. Paving a new path leads to a deeper understanding of who you are, not who you've been told to be.

When was the last time you tried something new?

Productivity requires communication, organization, and teamwork. Choose an efficient team that aligns with your work strategies and see great results! Do your part, and let others do theirs. Nobody needs to do everything...

Bees are social insects which live in colonies. There are three jobs in a bee colony: the queen, who lays eggs, up to 1500 a day, the drones, which are all male and do not work in the hive, their job is to mate with a queen to begin another hive, and the female worker bees take care of everything, especially the developing larvae you can see in this photo.

Do the people you work with really align with you?

Precision and focus can connect you to great things. Be aware of how you show up, and the effect you have on your surroundings.

Are you crystal clear on the life you desire to live?

Take time to examine small details, and notice the differences between things that at first glance seem the same.

Until it landed, this hoverfly looked like a bee. It mimics several characteristics of the wasp to be protected from predators. These beneficial insects feed mainly on nectar and pollen, but also eat aphids and other pests. If you see them, welcome them into your garden!

What is happening in your experience that could use a closer look?

Take what you need, and only what you need. Store what you will use, and share the rest. Know there is always enough. If you are ready for new things, let go of what isn't serving you and make room for new gifts to arrive!

When bees go from flower to flower, they take a small amount of nectar or pollen from each one. In the process of pollen collection, some is dropped as the bee travels from flower to flower, and cross pollination occurs so the plant can continue to produce seeds.

Can you see the resources available to you right now?

Devote your attention to one thing at a time and get to know it deeply, and intimately. Notice subtleties in your connections, and the gifts and lessons they bring. Let distractions go and see the truth!

Attraction and sensuality are an important part of the relationship between bees and flowers. Plants develop flowers so they can produce fruit, and seeds and continue to grow. Bees play a vital role in pollinating the plants, visiting the same type repeatedly to ensure the pollen gets distributed between flowers.

What are you attracting into your life?

Sometimes waiting is the only thing we need to do. It isn't time, the fruit isn't ripe yet, the buds of the flower aren't open, or it is the wrong flower entirely! Be patient, wait for the cues.

In general, bees aren't attracted to roses. The roses with numerous fluffy petals, don't have much nectar, and bee tongues aren't long enough to get to it anyway. They know roses aren't the best match for them, so they visit other flowers. Bees cannot see the color red, instead favoring blue and violet flowers, and their eyesight makes shades of yellow appear blue, so we often see them on yellow and orange flowers.

Can you tell when the fruits of life are ripe to pick?

Be with those who share your passions. Create together and allow wonderful things to unfold... Discover new places that enrich your life, and share them.

Are the people you spend the most time with supporting you?

Look right here in this moment, in this space, to find everything you need. It is already here waiting to be uncovered. Abundance is yours!

After a bee locates flowers, it returns to the hive and does a "waggle dance" in a specific pattern to tell the other workers where to go. The ebb and flow in nature ensures overall abundance, though we may see fluctuations happening, Nature knows everything is as it should be.

How often do you limit yourself with words like "can't, don't, shouldn't, and won't"?

If something isn't working for you, stop and approach from a different angle, then try again. Maybe even walk away for a day and come back with a new perspective.

Can you see your own life in the same way you'd watch a movie?

While we search and search for the big things, the smallest gifts sit unnoticed. Get up close and personal with things you normally walk past. There are entire worlds to observe!

What is in hiding right along the path you walk every day?

Sitting back and watching is an exceptional gift. Be aware of the situation as something outside of yourself, and also recognize how it relates to something occurring in your life.

An unusual moment captured as a lizard sat watching the bee on the path in front of it. In the time I watched, the bee got up, walked around a few times, then just stopped moving. The lizard's eyes followed the bee, head cocked to the side, but it didn't move.

Have you learned the art of observation without interaction?

Approach all things gently and touch them delicately. There is beauty in everything, waiting to be noticed. Leave everything you encounter as you found it, or better.

The relationship between flowers and bees is fragile and beautiful. The flowers stand out from the plants in a gorgeous display of color and send a gentle fragrance to attract bees, butterflies and other pollinators. They are rewarded with gentle touch of feet and proboscis tickling and probing their delicate blossoms.

Are you aware of how your touch feels to others?

We can achieve great things by approaching and interacting with our surroundings. The Earth is a school to explore, and you have an ALL ACCESS PASS! Ask to be gently showered with lessons and blessings and you will be!

Are you comfortable initiating a conversation with a stranger?

We are presented with countless opportunities. Choose wisely where to spend your time and energy. Everything is a lesson, and once the lesson is learned, you can move on to new things.

What have you been struggling to learn so you can let go of it?

You have chosen every aspect and situation in this lifetime so you can be free of limitations. Overcome all obstacles and let go of anything between you and your life! You are here to be amazing and powerful! Dive in, take that leap of faith and create your life!

Happy Birthday! The bee on the left is emerging from the comb and joining the hive! Bees know what they are here to do, and they do it well...

What are you here to create?

Light Tribe Earth Publications
www.lighttribeearth.com

www.ingramcontent.com/pod-product-compliance
Lightning Source LLC
Chambersburg PA
CBHW041527280526
45792CB00004B/1400